UNDERSTANDING SAND PLAY THERAPY

Unlocking The Power Of Sand Play Practices To Focus On Effective Techniques For Healing And Growth, Support, Nurture Emotional Well-Being In Children And More

DR. KARSON BRYAN

DISCLAIMER

This book's content is meant to be used solely for general informative purposes. Despite having taken every precaution to guarantee the content's accuracy, the author disclaims all duty and responsibility for any errors or omissions. It is recommended that readers exercise caution and, if needed, seek expert guidance. Any and all liability for losses, damages, or other outcomes arising from the use of the material included in this book is disclaimed by the author and publisher. All referenced product names and trademarks are the property of their respective owners and are merely cited for identification. Any likeness to real people or things is entirely accidental. Since it is a work of fiction, this book should not be used as a substitute for professional, legal, or medical advice. It is advised that readers seek advice on particular issues from qualified experts."

Please make sure that this disclaimer is modified to fit the particular requirements and subject matter of your book. Seeking advice from a legal expert is also a smart option if you have any questions or require a more thorough disclaimer for your specific book.

TABLE OF CONTENTS

CHAPTER ONE

SAND PLAY THERAPY

INTRODUCTION

A potent therapeutic strategy, sandplay therapy taps into the rich reservoir of creativity and symbolism found in the human psyche. It provides a singular and profound approach to individuals' inner exploration and healing, frequently beyond the constraints of conventional talk therapy. We will examine the history of sand play therapy in this introduction, as well as the key components of this therapeutic approach.

THE SANDPLAY THERAPY'S HISTORY

Sandplay therapy has its origins in the groundbreaking work of Swiss psychotherapist Dora Kalff, who was influenced by the well-known psychiatrist Carl Jung. In the 1950s, Kalff first came into contact with sandplay as a therapeutic technique and saw its potential to support self-expression and personal development. Motivated by the ideas presented by Jung regarding the collective unconscious and archetypal symbolism, she modified and enhanced sandplay to become a therapeutic approach.

A sandbox and little figures were used in Margaret Lowenfeld's "World Technique," which had a big impact on Dora Kalff's path into the field of sandplay treatment. But Kalff added her viewpoint and knowledge to this approach by fusing her knowledge of unconscious mind power with her grasp of Jungian psychology. She had a key role in transforming sand play therapy from its earlier forms into a more organized and therapeutic procedure.

THE CORE OF PLAY-BASED THERAPY

Sandplay therapy is fundamentally an integrative, symbolic, nonverbal type of psychotherapy. This method's key component is its capacity to access the deep and frequently concealed facets of the person's psyche. With the help of a tray full of tiny figurines and sand, the therapist crafts a sacred and safe area for the client. It is suggested that the client use these symbolic elements to paint images or landscapes that represent inner experiences.

By passing the constraints of language and reason, people can communicate directly with their unconscious through the sandplay technique. Clients use their underlying creative and intuitive abilities as they work with the sand and the little things. They can access, process, and integrate ingrained feelings, conflicts, and memories through this symbolic manifestation.

Moreover, sandplay treatment serves as a link between the conscious and unconscious minds. As the client explores the symbols and stories that emerge from the sandplay, the therapist acts as a witness and a guide. Through this cooperative process, the person can gain understanding, mend emotional scars, and progress personally and in terms of self-awareness.

Dora Kalff's groundbreaking work, which combined components from several therapeutic traditions to produce a singular and potent modality, is credited with giving rise to the concept of sandplay therapy. Sandplay therapy's fundamental strength is its ability to access the complex web of the unconscious mind, promoting profound healing and change. Through the use of creativity and symbolism, this therapy technique offers people a profound way to explore and heal their inner worlds. We shall go more into the tenets, methodology, and advantages of sandplay treatment in the ensuing parts.

CHAPTER TWO

THE EVOLUTION AND HISTORY OF SANDPLAY THERAPY

HISTORICAL BACKGROUND

Sandplay therapy is a special and inventive therapeutic approach with roots in psychology and psychotherapy that uses little figurines and sand as tools for self-expression and healing. It started as a type of nonverbal therapy in the early 20th century, which is where it all started. Although sandplay therapy has developed and gone beyond its Jungian origins, it is frequently linked to the more general domains of depth psychology and Jungian psychology.

IMPORTANT PEOPLE AND INFLUENCES

Dora M. Kalff, a Swiss psychotherapist, was a pivotal influence in the creation of sandplay treatment. During the mid-1900s, Carl Jung's theories regarding the collective unconscious, archetypes, and the individuation process had a significant impact on Kalff. Sand and small items could be used to help people access and explore their unconscious content, according to Kalff. She thought that this might result in a significant healing and therapeutic transformation. Her research played a key role in establishing the groundwork for modern sandplay treatment.

The genesis of sandplay therapy is influenced by Carl Jung's analytical psychology. The fundamental ideas of sandplay treatment were in line with Jung's emphasis on the symbolic character of the psyche and the significance of integrating repressed material. Through sandplay, clients can explore their inner world in a way that goes beyond verbal communication thanks to the use of symbols and archetypes.

EVOLUTION OF SANDPLAY TREATMENT

As psychology and psychotherapy have changed over time, sandplay treatment has also had to change and adapt. Although it has strong origins in Jungian psychology, it has also incorporated elements of object relations, attachment theory, and the transpersonal viewpoint. Sandplay therapy has become a more comprehensive and versatile modality for therapists as a result of the combination of many theories and practices.

The uses of sandplay therapy have grown beyond individual therapy in the hands of modern practitioners. These days, it's applied in a variety of places, such as group therapy sessions and even hospitals and schools. Sandplay therapy is a useful technique for working with a variety of individuals, from children to adults, and across many cultural and psychological contexts because of its versatility.

the evolution of sandplay therapy is an intriguing tale that began with the rich soil of Jungian psychology and progressed into a flexible and effective therapeutic modality. Its basis has been formed by its historical roots, influential people like Dora M. Kalff, and the influence of Jungian notions. Sandplay therapy has evolved, making it a useful and efficient approach for delving into the depths of the human psyche and promoting profound healing and self-discovery.

CHAPTER THREE

CONCEPTS AND FRAMEWORKS FOR THEORY

SANDPLAY AND JUNGIAN PSYCHOLOGY

Developed by Swiss psychiatrist Carl Jung, Jungian psychology is a well-known theoretical framework that delves into the richness and intricacy of the human mind. The idea of the unconscious mind and the investigation of the self via symbols and archetypes are fundamental to Jung's writings. Sandplay therapy is a therapeutic approach that is one of the applications of Jungian psychology. Sandplay is a distinct, nonverbal psychotherapy method that incorporates Jungian concepts and has become well-known in the counseling and psychology fields.

According to Jungian psychology, a person's ideas, feelings, and behaviors are greatly influenced by their unconscious mind. According to Jung, the unconscious is made up of both communal and personal components, the latter of which holds archetypal symbols that are universal to all cultures and eras. These archetypes, which can be found as symbols in stories, dreams, and artwork, are universal depictions of basic human experiences.

SYMBOLS AND THE UNCONSCIOUS

As a result of his research into the unconscious, Jung highlighted the significance of symbols in comprehending the human psyche. According to him, symbols serve as a gateway to the subconscious and the deeper levels of the mind, serving as the language of the unconscious. Symbols are more than just signs or representations; they have deep significance that goes beyond conscious, logical comprehension. They enable people to integrate and make sense of their inner world by providing a vehicle for expressing complicated, frequently contradicting facets of who they are.

Symbols can be used by the unconscious mind to express itself in a variety of ways, including dreams, fantasies, and creative works. These symbols might be quite personal, expressing a person's distinct feelings and experiences, or they can be archetypal, signifying ideas and themes that are shared by all people. To help clients develop self-awareness and psychological development, Jungian therapy frequently entails the investigation and interpretation of these symbols to obtain insight into the client's inner reality.

THE SAND TRAY'S FUNCTION

A key component of Sandplay therapy, the sand tray allows participants to create symbolic settings that are used as a container for unconscious inquiry. Fine sand fills the tray itself, giving clients a tactile and sensory material to mold and work with. Clients can place little figurines, objects, and symbols in the sand tray to create sceneries that represent inner thoughts, feelings, and problems. Through this procedure, the unconscious can be expressed concretely and visually.

A "blank canvas" on which the unconscious can project its contents is the sand tray. During the process of choosing and organizing symbols, clients use their nonverbal and intuitive abilities, overcoming the constraints of language and reason. The process of creating these sand scenes can unveil hidden facets of the personality, unsolved problems, and intense feelings, offering a wealth of material for investigation and understanding.

Sandplay therapy is a profound approach to exploring the human psyche and fostering psychological growth and healing. It is based on Jungian psychology. The sand tray transforms into a hallowed area where the unconscious is free to express itself, and the therapist is essential in assisting clients in deciphering and assimilating the symbols they make.

CHAPTER FOUR

SANDPLAY'S THERAPEUTIC PROCESS
DEVELOPING A THERAPEUTIC ALLIANCE

Building a solid therapeutic alliance is essential to the therapeutic process in the setting of Sandplay therapy. The basis for the client's inner world exploration with the sand tray and miniatures is this partnership, which is frequently referred to as a therapeutic alliance. Establishing a safe, accepting, and compassionate environment is essential to the therapist's success in developing a rapport and sense of trust with the client.

The therapist must be alert to the client's emotions, thoughts, and behaviors, and be genuinely present throughout sessions. This is showing empathy and unwavering positive esteem while actively listening to the client and supporting their experiences. When clients feel heard and understood, they are more willing to open up and join in the sandplay process.

PUTTING THE SAND TRAY IN PLACE

One important part of Sandplay therapy is the sand tray itself. It acts as a conduit for clients to examine and externalize their inner experiences. The actual arrangement of the sand, the selection of miniatures, and the overall aesthetics of the tray are significant. The clients have the freedom to select from a large selection of miniatures and arrange them in the sand tray to symbolize their inner conflicts, emotions, and thoughts.

The client should be able to express themselves freely without worrying about being judged in the setting that the therapist creates. Miniatures chosen and arranged might be used as symbolic representations of the client's inner life. The client's viewpoint and emotional attachment to the sand tray are ultimately what matter most, even though the therapist may offer direction or interpretation.

THE THERAPIST'S FUNCTION

In Sandplay treatment, the therapist has a special and important role to play. They support, encourage, and bear witness to the client's inside journey. The main duties of the therapist are to establish a secure and supportive space for the client, assist them in using the sand tray, and provide interpretations of the symbolic representations as needed.

The therapist also needs to have a thorough understanding of symbolic language and Jungian psychology. With this understanding, they can assist clients in exploring the subconscious parts of their minds and deciphering the meaning contained in the sandplay. It is imperative, therefore, that therapists avoid forcing their interpretations on their clients. They should instead support the customer in discovering their meanings and insights.

In addition, the therapist's duties include upholding professional boundaries, making sure the client is safe both physically and emotionally, and adjusting to the client's particular needs and pace. They must be aware of the client's weaknesses and prepared to handle any emotional problems that may come up along the way.

THE CLIENT'S FUNCTION

In sandplay treatment, patients take an active role in their recovery. Their job is to choose miniatures and arrange them in the sand tray using their imagination and sense of exploration. Clients can access and communicate their unconscious feelings, conflicts, and thoughts through this procedure.

Although this is a normal aspect of the therapeutic process, clients may not always instantly grasp the deeper meaning of the sandplay masterpieces they make. The sand tray's symbolic language gradually becomes more understandable as the therapist and client work together, and clients can learn more about their psyches. To help incorporate these realizations into their conscious consciousness, clients are asked to think back on and talk about their sandplay experiences with the therapist.

THE RECOVERY PROCEDURE

In Sandplay therapy, the healing process is a dynamic, complex journey. It entails the client's investigation of their unconscious, direction from the therapist, and the therapeutic alliance that fosters this investigation. Clients can externalize their inner conflicts and emotions through the creation and manipulation of the sand tray, which facilitates their exploration and resolution.

As clients continue to participate in the sandplay process, they may experience emotional catharsis, heightened self-awareness, and a deepening connection to their inner selves. The symbolism inside the sand tray can lead to significant insights and a sense of relief as clients obtain a greater understanding of their problems and conflicts.

The healing process is not linear, and clients may return certain themes or symbols in their sandplay over time. The therapist's role in this process is to provide a consistent and supportive presence, helping clients navigate their journey toward healing and self-discovery.

The therapeutic process in Sandplay therapy is built upon the establishment of a strong therapeutic relationship, the mindful setup of the sand tray, the roles of both the therapist and the client, and the complex, transformative healing process. This therapeutic approach allows individuals to explore their inner worlds through the use of symbols and creative expression, ultimately leading to a deeper understanding of themselves and a path toward healing and personal growth.

CHAPTER FIVE

MATERIALS AND SETUP

SELECTING THE RIGHT MATERIALS

When it comes to sand tray therapy, the selection of materials is a crucial aspect of the therapeutic process. The right materials can help create a safe and conducive environment for clients to explore their thoughts, emotions, and inner worlds. Careful consideration should be given to the choice of figurines, objects, and miniatures that will be available for clients to use in the sand tray.

Therapists typically curate a diverse collection of figurines and miniatures, including people, animals, plants, vehicles, buildings, and various symbolic objects. These items should be chosen with the client's needs and goals in mind. The therapist's selection of materials can reflect the client's age, interests, cultural background, and specific therapeutic objectives.

For instance, a therapist working with a child might include toys and figurines that are age-appropriate and relatable, while a therapist working with an adult might incorporate a more mature and symbolic selection of items.

The materials should also encompass a wide range of emotions and themes, allowing clients to express themselves in a meaningful way. Additionally, therapists should regularly assess and update their collection of materials to ensure they remain relevant and resonant with their client's evolving needs. An essential aspect of selecting materials is their quality and condition; broken or worn-out items may not be suitable for the therapeutic process and should be replaced to maintain the integrity of the sand tray experience.

PREPARING THE SAND TRAY

The preparation of the sand tray itself is a vital aspect of the therapeutic process in sand tray therapy. The tray serves as a blank canvas, a symbolic representation of the client's inner world, and must be carefully tended to create an environment conducive to self-expression and exploration. Several key considerations should be taken into account when preparing the sand tray.

First and foremost, the sand itself is a crucial element. The sand used in sand tray therapy is typically fine-grained and can be of various colors, including white, natural, or colored sand. The therapist may choose the type of sand based on the client's preferences or therapeutic goals. The sand should be evenly distributed in the tray, creating a level surface that allows the client to sculpt and shape it as needed.

The therapist should ensure that the sand tray is clean and free from any debris or contaminants. A dirty or cluttered tray can be distracting and disrupt the therapeutic process. It's essential to maintain a sense of order and simplicity in the tray, allowing the client to focus on their inner experience.

The size and shape of the tray are also important considerations. The tray should be large enough to accommodate the client's chosen materials and offer ample space for creative expression. Therapists may choose from various tray designs, such as square, rectangular, or circular, depending on what works best for the client and their therapeutic goals.

THE THERAPEUTIC SPACE

Creating the right therapeutic space is fundamental to the success of sand tray therapy. This space encompasses not only the physical environment but also the emotional and psychological atmosphere that the therapist cultivates to support the client's exploration and self-discovery.

In terms of the physical environment, the therapist should strive to create a calm, safe, and private space for the client. This includes comfortable seating, appropriate lighting, and a well-organized arrangement of materials and the sand tray. The therapy room should be free from distractions to enable the client to focus on the sand tray and their inner thoughts and feelings.

The therapeutic space should be characterized by an atmosphere of trust and non-judgment. Therapists should create a sense of emotional safety, encouraging clients to explore their inner worlds without fear of criticism or rejection. The therapist's empathetic and non-directive approach is vital in establishing this trust.

The therapeutic space should also be flexible and adaptable to meet the specific needs of each client. Therapists should be prepared to adjust the space based on the client's age, cultural background, and therapeutic goals. For children, the space may need to be more playful and child-friendly, while for adults, it should provide a sense of maturity and seriousness.

Ultimately, the therapeutic space in sand tray therapy is not just a physical location but a carefully crafted setting that fosters self-exploration, emotional expression, and personal growth. It is a place where clients can use the sand tray as a medium to connect with their inner selves and work through their challenges, guided by the therapeutic support and the symbolic language of the sand tray.

CHAPTER SIX

ASSESSMENT AND DIAGNOSIS IN SANDPLAY THERAPY

INITIAL ASSESSMENTS

Initial Assessments in Sandplay Therapy involve a thorough evaluation of the client's presenting issues, history, and current emotional state. This assessment is a crucial first step in understanding the client's unique needs and determining if sandplay therapy is an appropriate treatment modality. It typically begins with an initial intake interview, during which the therapist gathers information about the client's background, including family dynamics, personal history, and any relevant traumas or experiences. This information helps the therapist gain insight into the client's life and the reasons they are seeking therapy.

Additionally, the assessment phase involves observing the client's behavior, emotional expression, and interactions during the initial sessions. These observations provide valuable insights into the client's psychological state and their potential suitability for sandplay therapy. The therapist may also assess the client's level of comfort with symbolic expression and non-verbal communication, as these are key components of sandplay therapy. Understanding the client's readiness for this unique therapeutic approach is essential for a successful therapeutic process.

CASE FORMULATION

Case Formulation in Sandplay Therapy is a dynamic and ongoing process that integrates assessment findings into a coherent understanding of the client's psychological and emotional landscape. It involves synthesizing the information gathered during the initial assessment to develop a working hypothesis about the client's issues, internal conflicts, and therapeutic goals. This formulation helps guide the therapeutic process and provides a foundation for sandplay interventions.

The sandplay therapist uses symbols, images, and metaphors that emerge during the therapy sessions to refine their case formulation. These symbols often serve as mirrors of the client's inner world and can reveal unconscious material that requires exploration and processing. By continually updating the case formulation throughout the therapeutic journey, the therapist can adapt their interventions to the evolving needs and progress of the client. This dynamic approach is one of the unique features of sandplay therapy.

SANDPLAY FOR DIFFERENT POPULATIONS

Sandplay for Different Populations involves tailoring the sandplay therapy approach to suit the unique needs and characteristics of various client groups. While sandplay is a versatile therapeutic method, it can be especially effective for specific populations, such as children, adolescents, adults, and individuals with diverse cultural backgrounds. Each population requires a customized approach to make sandplay therapy accessible and beneficial.

For children and adolescents, sandplay can be an effective way to provide a non-verbal outlet for expression, allowing them to process complex emotions and experiences. The therapist may use a more directive approach, offering guidance and structure to help these clients access their inner world through the sand tray.

With adults, the therapist might employ a more open and exploratory approach, as they are typically more verbally expressive. Sandplay can complement traditional talk therapy by tapping into the non-verbal and symbolic aspects of the adult's psyche, enabling a deeper understanding of their inner conflicts and traumas.

When working with individuals from different cultural backgrounds, the therapist should be culturally sensitive and adapt sandplay interventions to align with the client's cultural beliefs and practices. This requires a respectful understanding of the client's worldview and a willingness to integrate their cultural symbols and values into the sandplay process.

Initial assessments in sandplay therapy lay the foundation for understanding the client's unique needs and readiness for the therapeutic process. Case formulation is an ongoing process that synthesizes assessment findings and adapts to the evolving therapeutic journey. Sandplay for different populations involves tailoring the approach to meet the specific needs of children, adolescents, adults, and individuals from diverse cultural backgrounds.

CHAPTER SEVEN

USING SANDPLAY IN CLINICAL SETTINGS

COMBINING SANDPLAY WITH ADDITIONAL THERAPEUTIC METHODS

To improve treatment success, sandplay integration into clinical practice entails combining this expressive and creative mode with other therapeutic modalities. A nonverbal and symbolic therapeutic method, sandplay therapy can be used in conjunction with other therapeutic modalities, including humanistic approaches, psychodynamic therapy, and cognitive-behavioral therapy (CBT). Sandplay can be used in conjunction with these strategies to give clients a comprehensive and adaptable therapeutic experience.

For example, using sandplay in CBT can be especially helpful for individuals who find it difficult to express their feelings and experiences orally. Through tactile and metaphorical play, people can externalize and explore their thoughts and feelings. To help clients better recognize and address cognitive distortions, trigger thoughts, and maladaptive behaviors within the framework of cognitive behavioral therapy (CBT), therapists can utilize a sand tray with miniature figurines.

On the other hand, the goal of psychodynamic therapy is to identify unconscious dynamics and tensions. By combining psychodynamic techniques with sandplay, clients can be helped to uncover and communicate deeply held feelings and unsolved concerns. The sand tray's symbolism and imagery might act as a conduit to the unconscious, offering insights into the client's inner world that conventional talk therapy would not be able to provide.

Humanistic therapeutic modalities place a strong emphasis on self-actualization and self-exploration, such as gestalt therapy and person-centered therapy. By giving people a way to create and engage with their inner world, sandplay can facilitate the process of self-discovery and foster personal development and self-awareness. The sand tray can be used by clients to investigate their values, strengths, and goals to eventually coincide with the humanistic concepts of self-acceptance and personal development.

Sandplay integration with other therapeutic modalities, however, also needs thought and training. To make sure that the integration is useful and cohesive, therapists must be well-versed in both sandplay techniques and the primary treatment model of choice. To accommodate each client's particular requirements and preferences, the therapist should also continue to use a flexible and client-centered approach.

DIFFICULTIES AND ETHICAL ISSUES

Sandplay therapy has several difficulties and ethical issues that therapists must deal with, just like any other therapeutic approach. To protect the well-being of both clients and therapists, these concerns must be addressed.

1. Maintaining client anonymity is an essential ethical consideration. Sandplay frequently results in the development of very intimate and symbolic imagery, thus it's critical for therapists to safely retain and safeguard their clients' sand trays and notes. To preserve the client's privacy, therapists should use caution while discussing the details of the sandplay sessions with other people.

2. Getting Informed Consent: Before using sandplay in treatment, it is imperative to get the client's informed consent. Clients need to comprehend the purpose of sandplay, how it will fit into their treatment plan, and any possible hazards or advantages that may arise.

41

3. Boundaries and Transference: Clients may have intense feelings and transference reactions when engaging in sandplay. To avoid any injury or exploitation, therapists need to be extremely watchful in establishing and upholding proper boundaries. To keep the therapy interaction safe and productive, it is crucial to address transference dynamics during the sandplay process.

4. Training and monitoring: To be used successfully, sandplay treatment calls for specific training as well as continuous monitoring. To make sure they are proficient in this technique, therapists should acquire advice from sandplay supervisors with experience and pursue further education.

5. Cultural Sensitivity: When utilizing sandplay with clients from a variety of backgrounds, therapists need to exercise cultural sensitivity. The significance of symbols and imagery might differ throughout cultures, therefore therapists

must be mindful of the possibility of insensitivity or incorrect interpretations.

6. Comfort of the Client: In the beginning, sandplay may be frightening or unsettling for certain clients. If sandplay is not a good fit for a client, therapists should be sensitive to the client's requirements and preferences and offer other therapeutic options.

7. Ethical Decision-Making: When integrating sandplay with other therapeutic techniques, ethical conundrums may come up. In addition to possessing a solid ethical foundation, therapists must be equipped to handle these situations by putting the client's needs first.

By providing clients with a distinctive avenue for self-expression and inquiry, sandplay integration into clinical practice can enhance the therapeutic process.

CHAPTER EIGHT

SANDPLAY FOR PARTICULAR PROBLEMS

A strong and adaptable therapeutic strategy, sandplay therapy can be used to treat a variety of specific difficulties, such as PTSD and trauma, grief and loss, anxiety and depression, identity and self-esteem, and family and interpersonal problems. Using a sand tray, tiny figurines, and a client's artistic expression, this therapeutic approach—which was created by Dora Kalff and based on Carl Jung's work—explores and processes deeply ingrained emotional and psychological issues. Sandplay therapy is a powerful way to address each of these ideas, providing people with a special, nonverbal way to heal and discover who they are.

TRAUMA AND POST-TRAUMATIC STRESS DISORDER

Both conditions can cause profound emotional scars that are frequently difficult to express. A secure and non-intrusive setting is provided by sandplay therapy for people to process their traumatic experiences. Clients can externalize and process their feelings by recreating situations, symbols, or emotions associated with their trauma in the sand tray. Healing and resolution can be facilitated by the building and manipulation of the sand as well as the symbolic depiction of their experiences through the figurines. Sandplay therapy promotes a sense of safety and control during the healing process by enabling people to access and express their trauma-related feelings and experiences in a non-threatening way.

LOSS AND GRIEF

Loss and grief are common emotions that can be exceedingly complicated. People can explore and express their feelings related to losing a loved one, a relationship, or even their sense of identity through the unique medium of sandplay therapy. With the use of the sand tray, clients can construct scenes and landscapes that mirror their inner emotional landscape, which helps them let go of repressed feelings and integrate their grief. People can externalize and explore their grief symbolically and creatively by working with small things and symbols; this helps them make sense of their loss and discover a way to recover.

DEPRESSION AND ANXIETY

Depression and anxiety can be overpowering and alienating. Sandplay therapy provides a concrete and artistic means of expression for those who are experiencing these problems. Clients can express their emotional states and investigate the root reasons for their anxiety and sadness by setting up little characters and situations in the sand tray. It can be beneficial in and of itself to shape the sand and place the figures in the tray; it fosters a sense of empowerment and control. In addition, sand playing helps people understand their emotional terrain, which in turn helps them create better-coping mechanisms and a stronger sense of self.

SELF-ESTEEM AND IDENTITY

Problems with these concepts can have deep roots and be difficult to resolve. A nonverbal way to explore one's self-concept and self-worth is through sandplay therapy. The sand and little figurines can be used by clients to symbolize several facets of themselves, including their weaknesses and strong points. Through symbolic processes, underlying ideas and conflicts about identity and self-worth can be revealed. Through active engagement with these representations, clients can get insights into their self-concept and strive towards a more affirming and genuine self-image.

RELATIONSHIP AND FAMILY ISSUES

Relationship and family issues can also be effectively addressed using sandplay therapy. People can draw symbolic depictions of their interpersonal difficulties, disputes, or family dynamics in the sand tray. This enables them to externalize and analyze these intricate relationships in a way that avoids conflict. Through the process of working with these symbols and figures, clients can discover more positive ways to relate to others and develop a deeper awareness of their role in relationships. In family therapy, sandplay can be especially helpful since it gives family members a safe, regulated environment in which to express themselves nonverbally and deal with their issues.

Sandplay therapy is an effective therapeutic strategy that can be customized to address a variety of problems, including trauma and PTSD, loss and grief, anxiety and depression, identity and self-esteem, and relationship and family problems. With the help of this nonverbal and symbolic approach, clients can work toward healing and personal development in a creative and safe environment while exploring and processing their feelings. Because of its special blend of symbolism and creativity, sandplay therapy is a useful tool in the toolbox of therapeutic interventions for a variety of psychological and emotional issues.

CHAPTER NINE

SIGNIFICANCE AND EXPLANATION
COMPREHENDING SANDPLAY SYMBOLS

Sandplay is a special and effective tool in psychology and therapy that enables people to explore and express their deepest feelings, experiences, and thoughts through symbolic play. The method is building a small globe or scenario in a sandbox with different objects, natural materials, and figurines. These carefully selected and positioned symbols frequently stand in for underlying feelings and tensions. Sandplay symbols are portals to the unconscious mind, so the therapist and the client need to understand them.

In sandplay, symbols can be anything from humans, animals, buildings, or natural elements. Each of these symbols has a complex, uniquely meaningful story associated with it. For example, one person may associate a simple tree figure with growth and a sense of connection to nature, while another person may associate it with a sense of loneliness and a link to the past. This demonstrates the extreme subjectivity of sandplay symbols, whose interpretation is firmly based on each person's own experiences and background.

INTERPRETING METHODS

Sandplay symbol interpretation is a difficult process that necessitates the therapist to maneuver through the complexities of the client's psyche. Several strategies are used to make this interpretation easier. Among the basic methods is active imagination. The client is urged to have a conversation with the symbols to investigate their significance through active imagination. This makes it possible to comprehend the feelings and experiences connected to the symbols on a deeper level.

Analyzing the positioning of symbols in the sand picture is another useful tactic. The placement, proximity, and arrangement of the symbols can reveal information about the internal dynamics of the customer. For instance, symbols that are close to one another can represent a struggle or a strong emotional connection, whereas symbols that are far apart might represent a sense of alienation or estrangement.

ELEVATION AND METAMORPHOSIS

The transcendence and transformation of the client's internal tensions and struggles are frequently the ultimate goals of sandplay therapy. People can face their unresolved issues, externalize their inner world, and ultimately find healing and wholeness through working with symbols.

When a client starts to view their concerns more broadly and gets insight into the fundamental causes, they transcend. This may result in a change in awareness and the discovery of fresh avenues for conflict resolution and personal development. During the sandplay process, the client may feel relieved, and released, and realize they have greater clarity.

On the other hand, transformation entails the person's genuine integration of healing and insights into their life. It denotes a profound shift in the person's beliefs, emotions, and actions. Sandplay symbols are essential to this transition because they serve as a means of bridging the conscious and unconscious minds, enabling the client to resolve internal problems and bring about positive life changes.

One of the most important parts of the therapeutic process is comprehending the symbols in sandplay. By deciphering these symbols using methods like active imagination and symbol location analysis, people can transcend and undergo metamorphosis, which in turn helps them comprehend themselves better .

CHAPTER TEN

TRAINING AND SUPERVISION IN SANDPLAY THERAPY

CERTIFICATION REQUIREMENTS

To become a proficient practitioner in the field of sandplay therapy, one must fulfill several essential training criteria. Play therapy, depth psychology, and symbolism are all combined in the distinctive and specialized field of sandplay therapy. As a result, to use Sandplay therapy properly, those who want to become therapists must complete a certain set of courses and training.

Completing a master's or doctoral degree in a related mental health field such as psychology, social work, counseling, or marriage and family therapy is the fundamental requirement for training in Sandplay Therapy. Students who complete this foundational course will have a strong foundation in general psychotherapy ethics and principles, which is an essential prerequisite for those who want to specialize in Sandplay Therapy.

To become proficient in Sandplay Therapy, prospective therapists must also take part in specific training courses. Comprehensive teaching on the principles and applications of Sandplay Therapy is provided by these programs. Coursework on the background of Sandplay, Jungian psychology, symbolism, and the useful application of Sandplay skills are frequently included in this kind of instruction. Reputable training facilities and businesses that specialize in sandplay therapy may provide these programs.

MONITORING AND ONGOING EDUCATION

Getting supervision and continuing education are essential to becoming a competent Sandplay therapist. Following the first instruction, people are usually expected to participate in supervised practice. Gaining hands-on experience and honing one's Sandplay Therapy skills requires this kind of supervision. To verify the therapist's competency and adherence to ethical principles, a certified Sandplay therapist or supervisor evaluates cases, provides assistance, and provides feedback during supervision.

Another essential component of keeping up one's skill in sandplay therapy is continuing education. Therapists must stay up to date on the most recent advancements, research, and best practices because the field is always changing. This may entail going to conferences, workshops, and additional in-depth training courses. Therapists who continue to study are better able to apply Sandplay strategies, broaden their clinical expertise, and maintain relationships within the Sandplay community.

OBTAINING CERTIFICATION AS A SANDPLAY THERAPIST

Practitioners usually have to fulfill certain standards and go through a formal certification process to become certified Sandplay therapists. A therapist's skill and commitment to Sandplay Therapy's ethical and professional standards are acknowledged by their certification.

One typical certification criterion is the fulfillment of a predetermined number of hours of practice under supervision. Depending on the certifying organization, the precise amount may change, however, it often falls between 100 and 400 hours. Under the supervision of a skilled supervisor, therapists use Sandplay techniques to work with clients during this time.

Certification may entail a written exam that evaluates the therapist's understanding of symbols, Sandplay theory, and associated psychological principles in addition to practical practice. A personal sandplay process, or a method of self-analysis employing Sandplay principles, may be required of therapists by certain organizations.

The therapist can seek certification through an accredited Sandplay Therapy association or organization once all requirements have been satisfied. The designation of Certified Sandplay Therapist (CST), which denotes competence and dedication to the practice of Sandplay Therapy, is bestowed upon the therapist upon successful completion of the certification process.

To become a certified Sandplay therapist, you must fulfill training requirements, get supervision, and pursue further education. While monitoring and continuing education guarantee that therapists keep their competence and ethical practice, training supplies the fundamental knowledge.